BUILDING
WORLD LANDMARKS

Arc de Triomphe

by Margaret Speaker Yuan

BLACKBIRCH PRESS

An imprint of Thomson Gale, a part of The Thomson Corporation

THOMSON
™
GALE

Detroit • New York • San Francisco • San Diego • New Haven, Conn. • Waterville, Maine • London • Munich

For more information, contact
Blackbirch Press
27500 Drake Rd.
Farmington Hills, MI 48331–3535
Or you can visit our Internet site at http://www.gale.com

LIBRARY OF CONGRESS CATALOGING–IN–PUBLICATION DATA

Speaker Yuan, Margaret.
  Arc de Triomphe / by Margaret Speaker Yuan.
    p. cm. — (Building world landmarks)
  Includes bibliographical references.
  ISBN 1-4103-0138-9 (hardback : alk. paper)
Summary: Discusses the Arc de Triomphe including why it was built, its construction and architecture, and the renovations and additions that have occurred up to the present day.
  1. Arc de Triomphe (Paris, France)—Juvenile literature. 2. Paris (France)—Buildings, structures, etc.—Juvenile literature. 3. Paris (France)—History—19th century—Juvenile literature. I. Title. II. Series.

  DC790.A6S665 2004
  725'.97'0944361—dc22   2004007017

Printed in the United States
10 9 8 7 6 5 4 3 2 1

Table of Contents

Arc de Triomphe

THE ARC DE TRIOMPHE stands at the heart of Paris, in the Place Charles de Gaulle, formerly known as the Place de l'Étoile (the Plaza of the Star). The plaza forms the hub of the great boulevards that radiate outward to the city limits. At a height of almost 165 feet (49.5 meters), the Arc de Triomphe is the world's largest triumphal arch.

The Arc was proposed originally in 1806 by Napoléon I, who ruled France from 1799 to 1815. During his reign, French forces intent on securing their borders fought a series of conflicts, called the Napoléonic Wars, against a coalition of English, Austrian, Swedish, and Russian forces. One of the greatest victories for the French during the Napoléonic Wars was the Battle of Austerlitz in what is now the Czech Republic. Napoléon envisioned the Arc as a monument and memorial to the French army's triumph in

Opposite: *During a parade celebrating Bastille Day on the Champs-Élysées, jets fly over the Arc de Triomphe, leaving vapor trails in the colors of the French flag.*

the battle. Preoccupied with continuing warfare, Napoléon fell from power before the Arc was built.

More than thirty years of war and political turmoil delayed the construction of the Arc. Finally on July 29, 1836, the Arc was inaugurated to honor the victories of the French army and to serve as a symbol of liberty. In the 1850s, Napoléon's nephew, Emperor Napoléon III, decided to rebuild Paris into a modern city. The prefect (city manager) of Paris, Baron Georges-Eugène Haussmann, used the Arc as the focus of the redevelopment plans. Twelve broad, tree-lined boulevards would begin at the Arc. Haussmann's plans turned the Place de l'Étoile into the city's centerpiece.

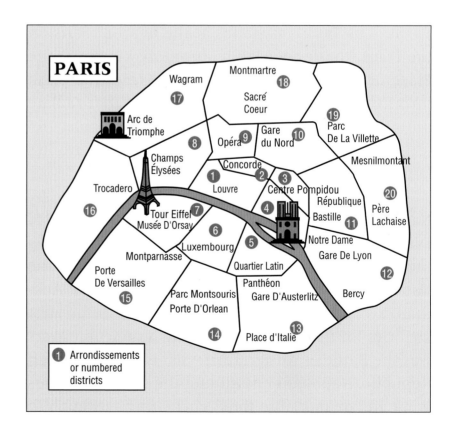

The Tomb of the Unknown Soldier and the Eternal Flame were placed under the Arc after World War I. Every year on November 11 (Veterans Day, known in France as Remembrance Day) and on July 14 (French National Day, similar to Independence Day in the United States), ceremonies are held at the Arc to commemorate the sacrifices made during wartime and to celebrate the ideals of the French Revolution: liberty, equality, and brotherhood.

French president Jacques Chirac (center) attends a 2004 ceremony held at the Tomb of the Unknown Soldier to mark the anniversary of the end of World War II.

Chapter 1

Napoléon's Vision

NAPOLÉON BONAPARTE WAS born the son of a minor nobleman on August 15, 1769, on the French island of Corsica. Destined for a military career, he was sent at the age of nine to the military academy at Brienne in France. After six years at Brienne, he attended the École Militaire (Military College) in Paris. Although the normal course of study took two years, Napoléon did so well at the Military College that he graduated in half that time. In 1785, when he was sixteen years old, Napoléon received his first commission, as a lieutenant in the artillery. He soon saw combat, where he showed himself to be fearless under fire and a born leader.

Napoléon's courage on the battlefield and his personal concern for his men won him the support of his soldiers. Napoléon, unlike other military leaders of his time, made sure that his soldiers were both paid

Opposite:
Jean-Pierre Cortot's sculpture, The Triumph of Napoléon, *is on the left face of the Arc, facing the Champs-Élysées.*

Emperor Napoléon Bonaparte's 1804 coronation is shown in this early-nineteenth-century oil painting housed at the Louvre.

and fed on time. "An army," he said, "marches on its stomach."[1]

In 1789, just four years after Napoléon's graduation from the Military College, the French Revolution began. The monarchy fell and was replaced with a republic. The king and queen, Louis XVI and Marie Antoinette, were beheaded in 1793. Napoléon fought in Italy, Sardinia, and Egypt until 1799, when he returned to Paris. Napoléon's soldiers, whom he had led and supported throughout many campaigns, in turn supported his political ambitions as he plotted to become France's ruler. As Napoléon said, "Revolutions are good times for soldiers of talent and courage."[2] Napoléon overturned the government and was proclaimed first consul. In 1804 he crowned himself emperor.

The Grande Armée

With the goal of securing France's borders, Napoléon amassed a huge army, the Grande Armée (Great Army). Fearful of Napoléon's prowess as a general and concerned that the French forces might overrun Europe, a coalition of allies formed to oppose him. The

After Napoléon's Grande Armée defeated coalition armies at the Battle of Austerlitz, shown in this painting, he proclaimed that a triumphal arch would be built in honor of his troops.

Grande Armée met the coalition armies at Austerlitz, at the time part of Moravia, in December 1805, where Napoléon's tactics and the courage of his soldiers won the battle against far greater numbers of soldiers and cannons.

The victory at Austerlitz demonstrated Napoléon's ability to outsmart and outfight his enemies. Napoléon, however, believed that the key to victory was his men and that glory for the victory was to be shared with the troops, with the privates as much as with the generals. Upon his return to Paris after Austerlitz, Napoléon issued an official proclamation: A triumphal arch would be built in honor of his troops, the Grande Armée. He intended it to be an enormous structure that would endure for thousands of years.

Plans for the Arc

Napoléon based his plans for the Arc de Triomphe on the Roman tradition of triumphal arches. The Arch of Constantine, built in A.D. 315 to commemorate the victories of Emperor Constantine, was the largest of the ancient Roman arches. Napoléon wanted the Arc de Triomphe to be the world's highest and most impressive triumphal arch. To achieve this goal, he proposed that it stand about twice as tall as the Arch of Constantine. Napoléon decided to build it in the Place de l'Étoile, one of the ancient entryways into the city of Paris. Locating the Arc there ensured that it would be visible from the entire city.

The plaza stood on a hill at the end of the Champs-Élysées (Elysian Fields), which at the beginning of the nineteenth century was a tree-lined park. The Champs-Élysées extended westward from the Place du Carrousel (Plaza of the Carousel) to the Place de l'Étoile. Napoléon's ideas for the design of the Arc included a roof balcony, accessible by a staircase inside the structure. The view from the roof of the Arc would be a panoramic one, since there were no other buildings as tall as the Arc between the Arc and the Louvre, the ancient palace built by the kings of France. At nearly 165 feet (49.5 meters), the Arc would be as tall as a twelve-story building.

Napoléon wanted his triumphal arch to be twice as tall as the Arch of Constantine (pictured), which had been built in Rome around A.D. 315.

Empire Style

Napoléon's influence extended beyond warfare and political power into the arts. He sought to create a style of decoration, clothing, and architecture that relied on the principles used by the ancient Egyptians, Romans, and Greeks. "Empire style," as it was known, featured simple lines, symmetry, balance, and restrained use of ornamentation.

In the decorative arts, objects such as tableware, desk sets, and furniture incorporated classic Egyptian, Roman, or Greek motifs. A common design for a paperweight, for example, was a miniature obelisk. These miniatures were made in imitation of the shafts of stone that Napoléon had seen on his campaign in Egypt. Furniture was decorated with small Greek columns carved into the woodwork. Tableware featured laurel wreaths and designs of classical gods and goddesses.

In women's dresses, the Empire style consisted of a short bodice with the waistline directly under the bosom. The long drape of the skirt from the waistline to the ankle showed the simplicity of line sought by Empire style designers.

In architecture, the Arc de Triomphe shows the classic lines of a Roman arch.

Empire-style dresses had short bodices, high waistlines, and long, graceful skirts, as seen in this painting of Pauline Bonaparte, Napoléon's sister, seated on an Empire-style chair.

The pillars are symmetric, and the ornamental sculptures are balanced and restrained. The sculptures are located in centrally framed pedestals, and they are highlighted by surrounding unadorned surfaces.

The Design of the Arc

A competition was held among the leading architects of France to determine the design for the Arc. Proposed designs included structures with columns set into the facades beside the arches, others with free-standing columns, some with an architrave (molding) around the building, some with a plain roof balcony, and some with a roof crowned by statuary, either of the goddess Victory in a chariot or of Napoléon dressed in his imperial robes. Some of the designs featured the names of generals and battles inscribed on the outside of the structure, while others placed inscriptions inside the Arc. Jean-François Chalgrin, a well-known architect who had worked on the Collège de France (College of France) and the Luxembourg Palace, won the competition.

Chalgrin's plan for the Arc called for a boxlike rectangular shape, about 145 feet (45 meters) long by about 70 feet (22 meters) wide by 160 feet (49 meters) tall. A huge arch, called the grand arch, would run through the center of the Arc on the long side of the rectangle. Two smaller arches would run through the short sides of the rectangle. Four rectangular pillars would support the grand arch, which would reach a height of about 100 feet (30 meters). Each pillar would occupy about one-third of the length on the long side of the structure, with the opening of the grand arch occupying the remaining third. On the short sides, the two smaller arches would reach a height of about 60 feet (18 meters). The vaulted ceiling of the grand arch would be covered with rosettes

The inside walls of the pillars of the Arc are decorated with inscriptions of generals and heroes of France, as well as other patriotic carvings.

and decorative sculptures. The inside walls of the pillars of the Arc would be embellished with inscriptions and patriotic carvings. An architrave would be placed around the outside of the Arc, at the level of the top of the grand arch. To house a museum, a large room, called the attic, would be built inside the structure, between the top of the grand arch and the roof. The architrave, the attic, and the roof would be supported by freestanding columns that flanked the arches, four on the long side of the rectangle and two on the short side. Inside the pillars would be space for staircases and for drainage. Statuary that represented Victory riding in a chariot would be placed on the roof. A roof balcony was also included, so people could view Paris from the top of the Arc.

Work Begins

Once Chalgrin's plan was approved, work could begin. The site was excavated to a depth of about 25 feet (8 meters) so that the foundations could be laid. Two abutments (supporting structures) consisting of stone slabs set into concrete were placed lengthwise underneath the monument. To support the enormous weight of the structure, sixteen more abutments (four per pillar) were sunk into the soil. The spaces between the abutments were filled with gravel.

Work on the abutments and foundations continued for nearly two years. On Napoléon's birthday, August 15, 1806, the first stone of the Arc was set into the ground in the Place de l'Étoile. By the end of 1807, the foundations reached street level, and work on the aboveground structure could begin.

Chapter 2

Delays and Obstacles to Construction

BUILDING METHODS AT the beginning of the nineteenth century differed very little from earlier methods, such as those used to construct the cathedrals and castles of the late medieval period. The Arc was built before steam power, before railroads, and before the invention of power construction machinery. Workers used plumb lines (cords with weights at the bottom) to measure vertical distances. Cranes and pulleys to lift the stones into place were operated by horse power. Block and tackle equipment, used for positioning stones precisely into line after they had been lifted, was operated by hand. Building materials were transported to the site by barge and cart. Humans and horses supplied all the power to forge iron, to move building materials, and to lift stone and mortar into place.

Scaffolding and Stone

The first step in building the aboveground structure

Opposite:
The Eiffel Tower can be seen in the distance in this night view of the triumphal arch that Napoléon envisioned would stand for thousands of years.

was to build the scaffolding. Scaffolding would support the Arc during construction and provide a working platform for the builders, building materials, and tools. The next step was to construct the hoists. A turnstile was built in the center of the site. Horses harnessed to the turnstile provided the power for the hoists. Ropes from the turnstile were attached to pulleys at the top of the scaffolding. As the horses pulled the turnstile, the hoists moved up and down, as needed. The hoists operated almost continuously during the day, moving tons of stone, mortar, brick, lumber, iron pipes, and tools.

In 1808 the government established a quarry for the stone to be used in the construction. Located at Château Landon, south of Paris on the Seine River, the quarry was the site of rich seams of limestone. The limestone, known as the royal bank, was homogeneous and high in quality. In addition, the quarry's location near the river allowed the heavy blocks of stone to be moved in barges along the river instead of by cart. The roadways at the time were unpaved and often treacherous. River transportation was far less expensive and far more convenient.

The stone itself was cut using ancient methods. The most common method for cutting individual blocks from the stone face was called "plug and feathers." A line of holes would be drilled by hand into the stone. A pair of curved steel wedges (the feathers) would be placed into each hole. A third wedge (the plug) would then be hammered between the pair of wedges to drive them apart. As the work-

ers hammered the plugs along a line of feathers, the block would crack along the line and split from the stone face of the quarry. Blocks were cut in roughly rectangular pieces that weighed about a ton. They would be moved along a series of rollers (round wooden pieces) and hoisted by hand-operated pulleys onto a mason's worktable. The mason would cut the rough stones into squared-off building blocks.

Once the blocks were squared off, they were hoisted down off the table and onto another series of rollers. They were rolled along to the dock and lifted onto a barge. Teams of horses harnessed to the barge

The heavy lime-stone blocks used to build the Arc came from a quarry south of Paris and were transported to the city on barges on the Seine River (pictured).

Sculptures and carvings decorate the top of the Arc and the roof balcony, from which tourists have a spectacular view of Paris.

walked along the riverbank and pulled the barge toward Paris. After the barge reached Paris, the stone was unloaded and sent to storage yards until it was needed.

The plan for the Arc called for iron to be used both decoratively and structurally throughout the Arc—in the drainage system, for the staircases, and for rails, fences, and decorations. Iron drains would be used to collect the rainwater that fell onto the roof. The water would be funneled into a downspout in the center of two of the pillars and channeled outside the Arc onto the plaza. The staircases inside the other pillars would be constructed of iron steps that spiraled around a central iron pole. Iron fences, gates, balustrades, and chains would be used to keep visitors away from the edges of the roof balcony and to close the structure to visitors after hours. The ironwork would be decorated with motifs representing sabers, crowns, and *croix d'honneur* (crosses of honor), the same symbol used in medals of valor given to soldiers for their courage.

Financial Problems

While the scaffolding and hoists were being built on the Place de l'Étoile, the Napoléonic Wars continued. Napoléon was preoccupied with battles and finances. The continuing warfare drained money from the French economy. Tens of thousands of men who would have been employed in the civilian sector of the economy joined the army instead. Many farms and businesses were left without enough workers to continue production of food and manufactured goods. As the economy began to stagnate, prices went up and shortages became common.

To save money, Napoléon halted construction of the Arc and stockpiled the stone. He also revised the plan so that the Arc would be smaller than he had originally intended. The architect, Chalgrin, suggested that the Arc's original height be kept, and that the columns be removed in order to save money. Chalgrin's suggestions prevailed, and the construction continued, but sporadically, depending on how much money was available after the army budget was met. Between 1807, when the foundations were completed,

Triumphal Arches

In ancient Rome, victorious generals received a "triumph" to celebrate their return to the city. The ceremony consisted of a parade along a specific route through Rome. The chiefs of conquered armies marched at the front of the parade, followed by the spoils of war, such as gold, religious symbols, or captives. Musicians performed along the parade route, which was decorated with flags showing warlike figures. The troops marched, followed by the general, who came last. He drove a chariot pulled by two white horses. A slave would stand behind the general, holding a laurel crown over the general's head. The slave repeated continually *"Memento homo."* ("Remember, you are only a man.") Amid a tumultuous welcome into Rome, the general was reminded constantly that he was only a man, not a god.

Modern triumphal arches evolved from the Roman celebrations. The Romans first built arches of fabric and wood that were dismantled after the triumph. Permanent arches, made of stone and decorated with bas-relief, began with the Arch of Titus in A.D. 81. In the medieval period, cities were often built with monumental arched gates in their defensive walls. These gates could be closed during warfare. The tradition of triumphal arches met the tradition of city gates at the Place de l'Étoile, where the Arc de Triomphe was built on the site of one of the ancient portals to the city.

Victory parades also evolved from the ancient custom of triumphs. Modern parades incorporate not only the ground troops but the air corps as well. Today, aircraft streaming plumes of blue, white, and red smoke cruise over the Arc on July 14 to celebrate the national ideals of liberty, equality, and brotherhood.

The Arch of Titus was built in A.D. 81 and was the first permanent triumphal arch.

and 1810, design and budget issues kept aboveground work on the Arc from beginning. Empty scaffolding stood on the plaza while stone, cut at the quarry and brought to Paris, stayed in storage.

Napoléon's Wedding

In 1810, however, Napoléon's wedding plans renewed his commitment to the Arc. For his triumphal entry into Paris with his bride, Marie-Louise of Austria, Napoléon decreed that a full-scale model of the Arc was to be built. Fabric covered the scaffolding and filled in the spaces that would later be constructed out of stone. The model showed how tall and massive the monument would be upon completion. After the wedding, Napoléon committed the necessary funds to finance the construction of the Arc. Despite the continuing sluggishness of the economy, Napoléon's plan to honor the army with the Arc de Triomphe went forward.

Stones from the stockpiles were loaded into carts and driven to the Place de l'Étoile. There, workers wearing the traditional garb of French laborers—a light blue smock, a neck scarf, baggy trousers, and a beret (the French cap)—moved the stones over a series of rollers off the tailgates of the carts. The first stones were rolled onto small, manual hoists and moved into place to form the bases of the pillars. The workers positioned the stones using the same kind of hand-operated pulleys that had been used in the stone quarry. Workers started at one corner and set the first level of stones into place. The pillars were built the

A print from the early 1800s shows Napoléon with his bride, Marie-Louise of Austria, entering the Champs-Élysées through a full-scale model of the unfinished Arc de Triomphe.

same way brick walls or brick chimneys were constructed, but instead of bricks, 1-ton blocks of limestone were used. As the stone pillars rose, carts delivering the stone blocks to the plaza drove to the center of the site, where the stones were rolled off the tailgates of the carts and directly onto the hoist. Each stone was then lifted as high as was needed, depending on how high the construction had reached. Workers stood on scaffolding and rolled the stones off the hoists. Each successive row of stones was positioned and mortared into place.

By 1814 construction on the Arc had reached 65 feet (19.8 meters), and work on some of the ornamental sculptures had begun. However, in 1815 Napoléon fought the Duke of Wellington, the leader of the English and Prussian armies, at the Battle of Waterloo. Napoléon was defeated and his empire was destroyed. He was sent into exile, where he died in 1821. In his will he repeated his motto: "Everything for the French people."[3]

Completing the Arc

WITH NAPOLÉON'S DEFEAT, the monarchy returned to France. Louis XVIII, the brother of Louis XVI, the last king, was crowned. France experienced an economic revival. Amid the new prosperity, the reminders of the Napoléonic Wars and of the emperor, such as the half-finished Arc, did not win favor with the new king or with the public. In fact, there was a popular movement to tear down the existing structure and to use the stones for other buildings. The Arc languished, incomplete and without funding, until 1823, when Louis XVIII decreed that the Arc would be completed and dedicated to his victories in the war with Spain that had just ended.

Work began again with the construction of the small side arches. Scaffolding up to this point had been positioned parallel to the external facades of the pillars. Now, new scaffolding was constructed across

Opposite:
Almost 165 feet tall, the Arc de Triomphe is the largest triumphal arch in the world.

After Napoléon was defeated in 1815, work on the Arc was stopped until 1823 when Louis XVIII (pictured) decreed that it would be completed and dedicated to his victories in the war with Spain.

the openings of the small arches, to support the stones that would create the arches. Where the curved section of the arch was to begin, workers built a central beam across the opening. From this central beam, a triangle of girders was constructed to support the stones of the arch. Workers hoisted the wedge-shaped side stones, called voussoirs, into place. Last, the keystone, the central stone of the arch, was lifted up to the top of the arch and slid into place. With the keystone in position, the arch stood on its own, and the support scaffolding could be removed.

The grand arch was constructed in a similar fashion. Because the grand arch would be like a tunnel, workers built a platform at the level where the arch would begin to curve, at about 80 feet (24.4 meters). Workers stood on the platform and built a line of supports for the voussoirs. They then constructed an unbroken series of arches to form the vault of the grand arch. By 1830, the construction of this vault, about 100 feet (30 meters) from ground level, was completed.

Delays and Changes to the Arc

Political stability remained an elusive goal under the monarchists. Attempts by Louis XVIII and his successor, Charles X, to rule as autocrats met with armed insurrections. In 1830, Charles X was overthrown. A constitutional monarchy, with strict limits on the powers of the king, was established, and Louis Philippe, a nephew of the royal line of French monarchs, was elected king. Under his rule the original vision of the Arc was restored. Once again it would be a symbol of the patriotic sacrifices of the Grande Armée, as Napoléon had intended. Louis Philippe's commitment to the Arc caused construction to proceed rapidly.

Between 1830 and 1836, the attic was built, the Arc was roofed, the staircases were completed, and the roof balcony's final design was approved. The overhang of the gutters above the pedestals was adjusted to ensure that the sculptures would be protected from rainwater. The surrounding field was paved, and drainage work was completed. Gaslights, the newest type of illumination, were installed.

While the construction continued from 1830 to 1836, the decorative sculptures were also being carved. The completed sculptures were transported one by one to the Arc in horse carts. Special toothed joints, designed so that the seams would be both very strong and completely hidden from view, were used to seat the carvings onto the facades of the Arc. As the Arc neared completion, the sculptures were draped with cloth to hide them from curious passers-by until the official opening ceremony for the Arc.

Sculpture and Decorations

At ground level on the eastern facade (closest to the center of Paris), on the right pillar, is the most famous sculpture of the Arc. It is a group of figures called *Departure of the Volunteers*, executed by François Rude, a prominent sculptor. In the sculpture, War was personified as a winged creature who held a sword and called the volunteers to enlist in the Army of the Republic. Also known as "the Marseillaise," the group received its nickname from the town of Marseilles, which was well known for the patriotism of its citizens. Many residents of Marseilles had volunteered for the Grande Armée. The town also gave its name to the French national anthem. The group formed the most visible symbol of patriotism on the Arc.

On the left pillar, a group of figures carved by the sculptor Jean-Pierre Cortot showed Napoléon being crowned by Victory. On the western side of the Arc, groups titled *Resistance* and *Peace*, both by the sculptor Antoine Etex, decorated the monument. Other bas-relief sculptures were carved into six caissons (boxes), two on each of the long sides of the Arc and one each on the short sides. In addition, friezes (decorative horizontal bands) and tympana (spaces between the arch and the squared-off bottom of the architrave) featured carvings of infantry, cavalry, artillery, and the navy.

Huge sculptures, bas-reliefs, carvings, and friezes decorate the massive Arc.

The ceiling inside the arch is covered with carved rosettes, and the walls are inscribed with the names of generals and the major battles of the Napoléonic Wars.

Inside the arch, the ceiling was covered with rosettes. The walls were inscribed with the names of major battles of the Napoléonic Wars, and with the names of the generals who commanded the assaults. Throughout the monument, the figures of the imperial eagle (symbol of the empire) and the rooster (symbol of vigilance in the protection of freedom)

were used. The group of statuary that was to be located on the roof as a crown for the Arc was determined to be too expensive to create at the time.

The Arc, in its final form, was a masterpiece of construction. Each of the four pillars supported twice the total weight of another Parisian landmark, the Eiffel Tower, which was constructed out of iron decades after the Arc was completed. At nearly 10 million pounds (4.5 million kilograms), the Arc was eight times heavier than the Eiffel Tower. Most of the weight of the Arc consisted of 1-ton stone blocks, nearly fifty thousand of them.

The Arc's Inauguration

On July 29, 1836, the Arc was inaugurated. It was the sixth anniversary of the establishment of the constitutional monarchy. The date symbolized, for Louis Philippe and for the Arc, the belief in democratic ideals that had led to the original French Revolution, in 1789. A huge French flag hung in the grand arch. Smaller flags decorated windows throughout Paris. The ceremony began with companies of soldiers parading down the Champs-Élysées and through the Arc. Precisely at ten in the morning, the cloths hiding the sculptures were removed. In the brilliant sunshine, the Arc gleamed radiantly white. Citizens danced in the streets in celebration of the ideals of the Revolution: liberty, brotherhood, and equality. After darkness fell, fireworks highlighted the new monument, the world's largest triumphal arch.

The Modern Arc: Centerpiece of Paris

DESPITE THE PATRIOTIC fervor of the Arc's inauguration, and despite the hope of many French citizens that the constitutional monarchy would prevail over continuing political unrest, Louis Philippe's popularity did not last. He abdicated in 1848 and the monarchy was replaced by the Second Republic, a democracy. Napoléon I's nephew, Louis-Napoléon, was active in politics in France. His election as president in 1848 proved to be the Second Republic's undoing. Louis-Napoléon suspended the constitution and established the Second Empire. He proclaimed himself Emperor Napoléon III in 1852.

One of Napoléon III's goals was to turn Paris into a modern city. By the middle of the nineteenth century, Paris was suffering the effects of more than two thousand years of haphazard growth. There had never been an urban plan, or building codes to ensure safe

Opposite:
Today the Arc de Triomphe stands at the heart of Paris.

construction, or any thought of traffic control. The city was full of decaying buildings, traffic jams, and unsanitary conditions. The upper stories of many buildings were wider than their lower stories, so that they jutted out or connected to other buildings over the narrow streets. The upper stories prevented light from reaching street level. Sidewalks did not exist. Small troughs carried wastewater and sewage down the center of the streets, which were little more than damp, dark tunnels. Illnesses such as cholera and tuberculosis were common.

A Modern City

Urban planning was invented by Napoléon III to solve these problems. Napoléon III, unlike his uncle Napoléon I, wanted to create a strong France through peaceful means rather than through warfare. Napoléon III's vision for Paris, together with that of the city manager, Georges-Eugène Haussmann, called for the Arc, the tallest monument in the city at the time, to become the axis around which the life of the city would turn.

Haussmann's redevelopment plan was not always popular. Many people were displaced from their homes, which were torn down in the first phase of the plan. Haussmann was widely reviled at the time for destroying large sections of historical Paris. Later writers, historians, and architects, however, gave him credit for the creation of one of the greatest boulevards in the world, the Champs-Élysées. During Haussmann's tenure as city manager, the Champs-Élysées was paved from the Place du Carrousel to the

Arc. Chestnut trees were planted beside the street. The corridor that started at the Place du Carrousel and ended at the Arc de Triomphe became a prototype for modern city life. It incorporated green space, a wide pavement for carriages (and, later, for automobiles), sidewalks, dining establishments, stores, and well-constructed, healthful living spaces.

By 1871, the redevelopment of Paris had largely been completed, but a question remained for the Arc: Should it be crowned with sculpture or not? Many proposals had been made in the years since the Arc's inauguration, with many different themes for the sculpture. Temporary plaster models had been placed on the roof of the Arc, but no permanent installation

This 1820 illustration by Leonard de Selva shows the Champs-Élysées from the top of the Arc de Triomphe.

had ever been funded. The debate about whether to crown the Arc continued into the twentieth century. Some architects and art historians felt that the uncrowned Arc had an unfinished look. Others believed that the undecorated roof balcony gave the Arc a blocky, massive appeal and increased its impression of monolithic strength.

The Modern Arc

In the twentieth century, the Arc's image as a monument to warlike patriotism began to change. As a result of the tremendous loss of life in World Wars I and II, the French government added symbols of remembrance and peace to the Arc. During World War I, more than 1 million French soldiers perished in the defense of their homeland. The remains of an unknown soldier were buried under the Arc on November 11, 1920. In 1923, the Eternal Flame was lit near the Tomb of the Unknown Soldier. To allow more visitors to reach the roof balcony, an elevator was installed inside one of the pillars in 1929.

During World War II, nearly 60 million people died worldwide. Parts of Europe were devastated by bombing raids. Northern France, including Paris, was occupied by the forces of Hitler's Third Reich. After the invasion of Normandy on June 6, 1944, forces of the Allies—mainly England, the United States, and France—swept south toward Paris. On August 24, 1944, the day Paris was liberated, citizens of the city flocked to the Arc to cheer the Allied soldiers who paraded through the structure.

In the years since World War II, the Arc has been renovated twice. From 1986 to 1989, to celebrate the bicentennial of the French Revolution, the outside of the Arc was cleaned and cracks in the structure were repaired. The scaffolding that surrounded the Arc became a work of art itself. Painted blue, white, and red by the artist Catherine Feff, the scaffolding resembled a huge French flag. The second renovation, in 2003, was more extensive

The Arc de Triomphe was repaired, renovated, and cleaned between 1986 and 1989 to celebrate the bicentennial of the French Revolution.

Every year more than 350,000 people visit the Arc that serves as a symbol of the ideals of the French Revolution: liberty, equality, and brotherhood.

and included cleaning of the ornamental rosettes inside the grand arch, refurbishment of the attic that housed the museum, and installation of a new elevator.

Changes, Additions, and Renovations to the Arc

Changes and additions to the Arc modified Napoléon's vision of the monument. At the time it was created, the Arc symbolized the glory of war. The addition of the Eternal Flame and the Tomb of the Unknown Soldier signified the remembrance of World War I. In the intervening years, the flame and the tomb have come to symbolize the sacrifices of all soldiers and all citizens in wartime, and of hopes for peace in the future. Ceremonies of remembrance are held at the Arc every year on November 11, the anniversary of the armistice that ended World War I. The Arc is the focus of the annual celebrations for France's National Day, July 14, a holiday that celebrates the beginning of the Revolution. The Arc is the hub of festivities that include fireworks, dancing in the streets, and parades along the Champs-Élysées.

The Arc today is the symbolic center not just of Paris but of all of France. More than 350,000 visitors every year climb up or ride the elevator to the museum inside the attic. From the museum they can climb a bit more to the roof balcony, where they can look down the avenues and up toward the Eiffel Tower in the distance. The Arc has become a visual reminder of the ideals of the French Revolution: liberty, equality, and brotherhood.

Chapter 1: Napoléon's Vision

1. Quoted in Napoléonic Guide, "Napoléon's Maxims and Quotes: On War." www.napoleonguide.com/maxim_war.htm.

2. Quoted in Napoléonic Guide, "Napoléon's Maxims and Quotes: On War." www.napoleonguide.com/maxim–war.htm.

Chapter 2: Delays and Obstacles to Construction

3. Napoléon Bonaparte, last will and testament, April 15, 1821, in Napoléonic Guide, "Napoléon Bonaparte's Will." www.napoleonguide.com/napwill.htm.

Chronology

1769 Birth of Napoléon Bonaparte.

1789 Beginning of the French Revolution.

1899 Napoléon Bonaparte becomes first consul.

1793 Execution of Louis XVI and Marie Antoinette.

1804 Napoléon Bonaparte crowns himself Emperor Napoléon I.

1805 Napoléon's victory at Austerlitz.

1806 Arc de Triomphe decreed, and foundation stones laid.

1807 Foundations finished, and aboveground construction begun.

1814 Napoléon defeated and sent into exile. Height of the Arc reaches 65 feet.

1815 French monarchy restored. Plan to tear down the Arc receives popular support.

1821 Death of Napoléon I.

1823 Arc plan changed to commemorate the recent war in Spain.

1830 Revolution against the restored monarchy. Constitutional monarchy established. Louis Philippe crowned ruler of France and decrees that the Arc be completed in fulfillment of Napoléon I's original vision.

1836 Completion of the Arc and dedication on July 29.

1848 Louis-Napoléon, nephew of Napoléon I, elected president.

1852 Louis-Napoléon crowned Emperor Napoléon III, ruler of the Second Empire.

1853 Renovation of Paris under Baron Haussmann.

1871 End of renovation of Paris under Haussmann.

1920 Tomb of the Unknown Soldier placed under the Arc.

1923 Eternal Flame lit under the Arc on November 11.

1929 Elevator installed at the Arc.

1970 Place de l'Étoile renamed Place Charles de Gaulle.

2003 Restoration of the Arc begun.

Glossary

abutments—Supporting structures for the arches.

Arc de Triomphe—Arch of Triumph.

architrave—Molding.

bas–relief—Sculptures that project only slightly from the surrounding plane surface, without undercutting.

beret—French cap.

caissons—Decorative boxes.

croix d'honneur—Crosses of honor, in the same shape as the crosses given as medals for valor in battle.

Collège de France—College of France.

École Militaire—Military College.

friezes—Decorative horizontal bands.

Grande Armée—Great Army.

imperial eagle—Symbol of the empire.

Place de l'Étoile—Plaza of the Star.

plug and feathers—Technique for splitting stone.

plumb line—Cord with a weight at the bottom.

prefect—City manager.

rollers—Round wooden pieces used for moving stone building blocks short distances.

tympana—Spaces between the arch and the squared-off bottom of the architrave.

Remembrance Day—Veterans Day, November 11.

voussoirs—Wedge-shaped segments of an arch.

Books

Roxie Munro, *The Inside-Outside Book of Paris.* New York: Dutton, 1992.

Nancy Plain, *Louis XVI, Marie-Antoinette and the French Revolution.* New York: Benchmark/Marshall Cavendish, 2002.

Carol Strickland, *The Annotated Arch: History of Architecture.* Kansas City, MO: Andrews McMeel, 2001.

Web Sites

Discover France (www.discoverfrance.net/France/Paris/ Monuments-Paris/Arc-CDG.shtml#). Historic photos, description of pedestrian access to the Arc, and a capsule history.

French Monument Site (www.monum.fr/m_arc/ indexa.dml?lang=en). Short history of the Arc; information about visiting the Arc.

Paper Model (http://bj.canon.con.jp/english/3D-papercraft/building/index22.html). Download, print, cut out, and construct a paper model of the Arc.

View from the Top of the Arc (www.insecula.com/ salle/MS01729.html). Photos of the view from the top of the Arc looking down the boulevards.

Index